My

GRATITUDE
JOURNAL

The Complete Guide
To Cultivate an Attitude
Of Gratitude

*An Inspirational Journal
for Women to
Practice Gratitude*

WHY START A GRATITUDE JOURNAL?

We sometimes forget that gratitude is that special something that opens our hearts and connects our inner energy with more blessings. Being thankful for what we have and for the privilege to enjoy this experience called life is the key to open more doors and to receive more blessings.

By showing and expressing each day appreciation for all our blessings we attract more and more positive things to our lives. This wonderful gratitude journal is designed as a guide to make it easy for you to count and write down your daily blessings. This journal will serve its purpose as a reminder of all the things that are often overlooked and that we take for granted.

When we express gratitude, we improve our psychological wellbeing and our mental health. An attitude of gratitude helps us reduce a myriad of toxic feelings and emotions. Gratitude brings happiness into our lives and it helps reduce depression.

When we express gratitude daily we get in tune with a higher level of energy that paves the way to a more fulfilling life full of positivity. Gratitude can also help us repel all the negativity that surrounds us, and it reminds us to live in the moment and to be happy with what we already have.

Gratitude also reduces stress since you no longer feel the need to compare yourself with others. With gratitude you acknowledge that everything you need is already inside you. Expressing gratitude also enhances your self-esteem.

This journal is an invitation to focus on what you already have while you conquer all you want, it is a reminder of the importance of daily appreciation of all your blessings. Write every day everything you are grateful for until it becomes a habit. In this journal you can always write a list of all positive events you have each day.

This daily exercise will boost your appreciation for life and your self-esteem, you will feel more positive each day. Focus on the positive side of life while writing your gratitude journal. Gratitude works its magic when we write down all our blessings, it is the best antidote to get rid of all negative emotions.

We hope you enjoy your new Gratitude Journal,

Day: _____ Date: __ / __ / __

Today I am Grateful For:

_____

_____

_____

_____

_____

_____

"Feeling gratitude and not expressing it is like wrapping a present and not giving it." ~ William Arthur Ward

Day: _____ Date: __ / __ / __

Today I am Grateful For:

_____

_____

_____

_____

_____

One of the best ways to practice gratitude is to keep a gratitude journal. But how do you get started?

To make it easier for you to start your gratitude journal here is a list of prompts that will give you ideas:

1. Start writing about things or moments that make you feel grateful
2. Think about that special something that you made recently that make you feel happy and grateful
3. Look at everything that surrounds you and think about all those things that make you feel well and happy

"It is impossible to feel grateful and depressed in the same moment."
~ Naomi Williams

4. Think about what is that special something that you enjoy everyday that you often overlook and that makes you feel happy
5. Think about your qualities, your skills. What are those special qualities and skills that make you a unique person and who you are
6. Think about what you have learned from your mistakes
7. Think about all your accomplishments and how they have changed your life
8. Think about those friends or family members that have made your life better
9. Think about those books that you have read that helped you grow

Day:_____ Date:__ /__ /__

Today I am Grateful For:

_____
_____
_____
_____
_____
_____
_____

"Gratitude is not only the greatest of virtues, but the parent of all the others." ~ Cicero

Day:_____ Date:__ /__ /__

Today I am Grateful For:

_____
_____
_____
_____
_____
_____

How to Cultivate and Practice Gratitude?

Gratitude is appreciating what we already have instead of just looking for something external that we may not have in the hopes it will make us happier. The truth is that we can be happy with what we already have in this very moment if we learn to appreciate our blessings. We don't need to constantly get more things to feel satisfied, we don't need to constantly be praised to feel happy.

Gratitude is simply that attitude that makes it easy to feel good with our current situation, we should always feel joy now for what we have instead of what we lack. Gratitude can be understood as a mental state that grows even stronger when we practice gratitude. So, what is the best way to cultivate an attitude of gratitude?

"The smallest act of kindness is worth more than the grandest intention." ~ Oscar Wilde

The following are some of the ways in which one can practice and cultivate gratitude:

Express gratitude verbally and in written form. Every time you feel appreciation for something in your life, let that person or that group of persons know how you feel by expressing your emotions. This can be done with a thank you note that can be sent to that special someone that made your life even more meaningful or simply by saying to others how much you appreciate their help.

Always count your blessings. It is easy to forget and to overlook all the blessings that we enjoy every day because we are just so use to them and we take them for granted. Try to be present in the moment and acknowledge your current blessing like being able to breathe, being able to think freely and being able to enjoy life. Everybody has their own blessings, you just need to think about those beautiful simple things that make you a happier person every day. Write down those blessings every day.

"Gratitude turns what we have into enough" – **Melody Beattie**

Meditate. Meditation and especially mindfulness mediation means to focus on your present moment without worries. Just focus on those external factors that we take for granted like the sun, the breeze or the sounds of nature that make us feel happier and give thanks for having them. Feel the moment, feel the air that surrounds you, feel every sound that surrounds you and rejoice with the effects they cause in your mind. **Connect with nature as often as you can** and breathe thoroughly while you feel the joy of being alive in this beautiful world. We are the only ones who can make the world around us beautiful for ourselves with gratitude.

Don't forget to **read a gratitude quote every time you feel you need that reassurance** to feel grateful. Reading these quotes out loud will help you reinforce your feelings of gratitude.

Lastly don't forget to **keep a gratitude journal**. This is powerful and very effective to practice gratitude each day. Make it a habit to write down your thoughts and your blessings about all you enjoy every day. This will make a happier and more positive human being.

Always remember that gratitude just gives more meaning to your life and it makes you a happier and healthier person that enjoys life. Love your life, love your blessings and always be grateful. With gratitude you acknowledge the good in your life and you reject negativity.

Think about that someone that helped you get where you are right now. Our thoughts have energy and they also have power. Just thinking about the gratitude you feel, will send waves of good energy to that special person that made you feel special.

"No duty is more urgent than that of returning thanks." ~ James Allen

Day:_____   Date:___ /___ /___

Today I am Grateful For:

_____

_____

_____

_____

_____

_____

"Everything you can imagine is real" – Pablo Picasso

Day:_____   Date:___ /___ /___

Today I am Grateful For:

_____

_____

_____

_____

_____

Day: _____ Date: __ / __ / __

Today I am Grateful For:

_____
_____
_____
_____
_____

"The attitude of gratitude is the highest yoga." — Yogi Bhajan

Day: _____ Date: __ / __ / __

Today I am Grateful For:

_____
_____
_____
_____
_____

Day:_____ Date:__ /__ /__

Today I am Grateful For:

_____

_____

_____

_____

_____

_____

"The best dreams happen when you're awake." – Cherie Gilderbloom

Day:_____ Date:__ /__ /__

Today I am Grateful For:

_____

_____

_____

_____

_____

Day:_____ Date:__ / __ / __

Today I am Grateful For:

_____
_____
_____
_____
_____
_____
_____

"Walk as if you are kissing the Earth with your feet." — Thich Nhat Hanh

Day:_____ Date:__ / __ / __

Today I am Grateful For:

_____
_____
_____
_____
_____

Day:_____ Date:___ /___ /___

Today I am Grateful For:

_____

_____

_____

_____

_____

_____

"The things that we love tell us what we are." – Thomas Aquinas

Day:_____ Date:___ /___ /___

Today I am Grateful For:

_____

_____

_____

_____

_____

Day:_____   Date:___ /___ /___

Today I am Grateful For:

_____

_____

_____

_____

_____

_____

"Somewhere, something incredible is waiting to be known." – Carl Sagan

Day:_____   Date:___ /___ /___

Today I am Grateful For:

_____

_____

_____

_____

_____

Day:_____ Date:__ /__ /__

Today I am Grateful For:

_____

_____

_____

_____

_____

_____

"An attitude of gratitude brings great things." — Yogi Bhajan

Day:_____ Date:__ /__ /__

Today I am Grateful For:

_____

_____

_____

_____

_____

Day:_____ Date:__ /__ /__

Today I am Grateful For:

_____

_____

_____

_____

_____

_____

"If you can dream it, you can do it" – Walt Disney

Day:_____ Date:__ /__ /__

Today I am Grateful For:

_____

_____

_____

_____

_____

Day: _____ Date: __ /__ /__

Today I am Grateful For:

_____
_____
_____
_____
_____
_____

"The secret of getting ahead is getting started." – Mark Twain

Day: _____ Date: __ /__ /__

Today I am Grateful For:

_____
_____
_____
_____

Day: _____ Date: __ / __ / __

Today I am Grateful For:

_____

_____

_____

_____

_____

_____

"Believe you can and you're halfway there" – Theodore Roosevelt

Day: _____ Date: __ / __ / __

Today I am Grateful For:

_____

_____

_____

_____

_____

Day: _____ **Date:** __ / __ / __

Today I am Grateful For:

_____

_____

_____

_____

_____

_____

"What you do today can improve all your tomorrows." – Ralph Marston

Day: _____ **Date:** __ / __ / __

Today I am Grateful For:

_____

_____

_____

_____

_____

Day:_____ Date:__ /__ /__

Today I am Grateful For:

_____
_____
_____
_____
_____
_____

"It does not matter how slowly you go as long as you do not stop" – Confucius

Day:_____ Date:__ /__ /__

Today I am Grateful For:

_____
_____
_____
_____
_____

How to Unleash the Power of Gratitude

Being grateful gives us power, the power to transform our everyday lives into something magical and meaningful. We sometimes live our lives in this frenetic pursue of success without thinking about the beauty and the positive energy that surround us all the time. We as humans can make a choice, the choice to absorb and give all the good energy that is right there in the universe or simply turn into negative beings. Gratitude can help us reach and absorb that positive energy, we just need to be aware of our surroundings and be grateful for what we already enjoy and have.

"If you only say one prayer in a day, make it thank you." — Rumi

We have the ability to appreciate life in a beautiful way just by being present in the moment and by not focusing on our misfortunes. What our minds focus on expands and grows and it is precisely by being present in each moment that we can see the beauty of our world. The beautiful smile of a boy, the amazing beauty of a flower and nature or the privilege of waking up each day with a lucid mind are just a few examples of our countless blessings. To unleash the power of gratitude start practicing appreciation for what surrounds you and for that inner positive energy that you already own.

"When I started counting my blessings, my whole life turned around." – Willie Nelson

The very moment you start being aware of your blessings is the very moment you start unleashing the power of gratitude. Open your eyes and your soul to the gifts of nature and to the gifts of life. You are already perfect in your own way and you will start feeling more powerful and happy the moment you recognize that your inner energy can reconnect with the universal energy with the power of gratitude.

Love yourself and admire all your qualities, you are a fountain of positive energy and you can unleash the power inside you with gratitude. Write down all your blessings, all your qualities every day and get in constant contact with nature. Being surrounded by nature can unlock all that inner power you possess and can help us reconnect with our creative energy.

"Acknowledging the good that you already have in your life is the foundation for all abundance." – Eckhart Tolle

From now on start thinking that every day is a special day and not just another day. Yes, it is true, we sometimes tend to live our lives in autopilot and we forget the miracle of life and we forget that every new day can be special if we just practice gratitude. This new habit has tremendous power and writing down all your positive thoughts in your gratitude journal will help you unleash this power and will help you to be present in the moment.

"I was complaining that I had no shoes till I met a man who had no feet." — Confucius

"Be thankful for what you have; you'll end up having more. If you concentrate on what you don't have, you will never, ever have enough."
– Oprah Winfrey

To many people live their lives constantly waiting for that special moment to arrive, that special moment is right here, right now, each and every new beautiful day. All you need to be happy and to feel your inner power is right here with you, you just need to unleash that power with every day gratitude.

Also remember that our thoughts have energy and we can choose to be immerse in a spiral of negativity or in a world of beauty and abundance if we just choose the path of everyday gratitude. Find perspective and see everything in perspective, your life is already beautiful, you just need to see your current problems in perspective and learn to appreciate your present moment and present blessings. Look to the world around you with eyes of wonder and let all that energy flow inside your spirit, we are souls of energy and we receive that energy through gratitude.

"There are always flowers for those who want to see them." —
Henri Matisse

"A goal without a plan is just a wish." – Antoine de Saint-Exupery

Appreciate a sunset, grasp the beautiful moment of a sunrise, listen to the sounds of nature as often as you can, connect with your inner soul and smile with joy for that you already have. Just take a step back and stop what you are doing and take that walk through nature, enjoy your alone time and don't forget to write down your blessings in your gratitude journal to write in. Sharing these thoughts and habits can also unleash the power of gratitude, by sharing your gratitude thoughts you inspire others to join you in a wonderful gratitude movement.

"Gratitude is not only the greatest of virtues, but the parent of all the others."

– Marcus Tullius Cicero

Day:_____ Date:__ /__ /__

Today I am Grateful For:

_____
_____
_____
_____
_____
_____

"All things are possible if you believe"

Day:_____ Date:__ /__ /__

Today I am Grateful For:

_____
_____
_____
_____

Day:_____ Date:__ /__ /__

Today I am Grateful For:

_____
_____
_____
_____
_____
_____

"Problems are not stop signs, they are guidelines."- Robert H. Schuller

Day:_____ Date:__ /__ /__

Today I am Grateful For:

_____
_____
_____
_____
_____

Day:_____ Date:__ /__ /__

Today I am Grateful For:

_____

_____

_____

_____

_____

"You are stronger then you think"

Day:_____ Date:__ /__ /__

Today I am Grateful For:

_____

_____

_____

_____

Day:_____ Date:__ /__ /__

Today I am Grateful For:

_____
_____
_____
_____
_____
_____

"The mind is everything. What you think you become." – Buddha

Day:_____ Date:__ /__ /__

Today I am Grateful For:

_____
_____
_____
_____
_____

Day:_____ Date:___ /___ /___

Today I am Grateful For:

_____

_____

_____

_____

_____

_____

"Wherever you go, go with all your heart" – Confucius

Day:_____ Date:___ /___ /___

Today I am Grateful For:

_____

_____

_____

_____

Day:_____ **Date:**___ /___ /___

Today I am Grateful For:

_____
_____
_____
_____
_____
_____

"When I let go of what I am, I become what I might be." – Lao Tzu

Day:_____ **Date:**___ /___ /___

Today I am Grateful For:

_____
_____
_____
_____
_____

Day:_____ Date:__ /__ /__

Today I am Grateful For:

_____

_____

_____

_____

_____

"If you want to lift yourself up, lift up someone else." – Booker T.
Washington

Day:_____ Date:__ /__ /__

Today I am Grateful For:

_____

_____

_____

_____

Day:_____ Date:__ /__ /__

Today I am Grateful For:

_____
_____
_____
_____
_____
_____

"Gratitude is an opener of locked-up blessings." — Marianne Williamson

Day:_____ Date:__ /__ /__

Today I am Grateful For:

_____
_____
_____
_____
_____

Day:_____   Date:__ /__ /__

Today I am Grateful For:

_____
_____
_____
_____
_____
_____

"There are only two ways to live your life. One is as though nothing is a miracle. The other is as though everything is a miracle" — Albert Einstein

Day:_____   Date:__ /__ /__

Today I am Grateful For:

_____
_____
_____
_____

Day:_____ Date:__ /__ /__

Today I am Grateful For:

_____
_____
_____
_____
_____
_____

"Let us be grateful to the people who make us happy; they are the charming
gardeners who make our souls blossom" — Marcel Proust

Day:_____ Date:__ /__ /__

Today I am Grateful For:

_____
_____
_____
_____
_____

Day:_____ Date:__ /__ /__

Today I am Grateful For:

_____

_____

_____

_____

_____

_____

"Gratitude is the sign of noble souls." — Aesop

Day:_____ Date:__ /__ /__

Today I am Grateful For:

_____

_____

_____

_____

_____

Day:_____ Date:__ /__ /__

Today I am Grateful For:

_____
_____
_____
_____
_____
_____
_____

"Once you choose hope, anything's possible." – Christopher Reeve

Day:_____ Date:__ /__ /__

Today I am Grateful For:

_____
_____
_____
_____
_____

Day:_____ Date:__ /__ /__

Today I am Grateful For:

_____

_____

_____

_____

_____

_____

_____

"Don't regret the past, just learn from it." – Ben Ipock

Day:_____ Date:__ /__ /__

Today I am Grateful For:

_____

_____

_____

_____

_____

Day:_____ Date:__ /__ /__

Today I am Grateful For:

_____
_____
_____
_____
_____
_____

"Live what you love." – Jo Deurbrouck

Day:_____ Date:__ /__ /__

Today I am Grateful For:

_____
_____
_____
_____

Day: _____ Date: __ / __ / __

Today I am Grateful For:

_____

_____

_____

_____

_____

_____

"Whoever is happy will make others happy too." – Anne Frank

Day: _____ Date: __ / __ / __

Today I am Grateful For:

_____

_____

_____

_____

Day: _____ **Date:** __ / __ / __

Today I am Grateful For:

_____
_____
_____
_____
_____
_____

"Your big opportunity may be right where you are now." – Napoleon Hill

Day: _____ **Date:** __ / __ / __

Today I am Grateful For:

_____
_____
_____
_____
_____

Day:_____ Date:___ /___ /___

Today I am Grateful For:

_____

_____

_____

_____

_____

_____

"Wear gratitude like a cloak and it will feed every corner of your life." —
Rumi

Day:_____ Date:___ /___ /___

Today I am Grateful For:

_____

_____

_____

_____

Day:_____ Date:__ /__ /__

Today I am Grateful For:

_____

_____

_____

_____

_____

_____

"I'm grateful for always this moment, the now, no matter what form it takes." — Eckhart Tolle

Day:_____ Date:__ /__ /__

Today I am Grateful For:

_____

_____

_____

_____

_____

Day: _____ Date: __ / __ / __

Today I am Grateful For:

_____

_____

_____

_____

_____

_____

_____

"O Lord that lends me life, Lend me a heart replete with thankfulness!" —
William Shakespeare

Day: _____ Date: __ / __ / __

Today I am Grateful For:

_____

_____

_____

_____

_____

Day:_____ **Date:** __ / __ / __

Today I am Grateful For:

_____

_____

_____

_____

_____

_____

"Gratitude unlocks all that's blocking us from really feeling truthful, really feeling authentic and vulnerable and happy." — Gabrielle Bernstein

Day:_____ **Date:** __ / __ / __

Today I am Grateful For:

_____

_____

_____

_____

_____

Day:_____ Date:__ /__ /__

Today I am Grateful For:

_____

_____

_____

_____

_____

_____

"After a storm comes a calm." – Matthew Henry

Day:_____ Date:__ /__ /__

Today I am Grateful For:

_____

_____

_____

_____

Day:_____ Date:__ /__ /__

Today I am Grateful For:

_____

_____

_____

_____

_____

"Either I will find a way, or I will make one." – Philip Sidney

Day:_____ Date:__ /__ /__

Today I am Grateful For:

_____

_____

_____

_____

_____

The Importance of Gratitude in Life

Gratitude can simply be defined as thankfulness, figuring out simple happy moments, counting your blessings and acknowledging everything that you receive.

It is extremely important for every human being who wants to feel happy and fulfilled to practice gratitude. If you can practice gratitude, you would feel that everything in your life is a miracle. In addition, you will always be aware of how much you have been given.

Gratitude is so powerful that it can enhance and increase the quality of your life just by acknowledging all those little things that make you feel happy every day. You are only given one life and it is up to you to take the necessary steps to enhance its quality. That's why you need to learn how to be grateful and practice gratitude starting from today.

"Don't count the days, make the days count." – Muhammad Ali

Gratitude can help you reach your goals easily

Gratitude can literally transform your life. To fully achieve all your dreams, the practice of gratitude can help you realize your hopes and desires. Why? Because with gratitude you not only acknowledge all the power that you already have inside you, you also enjoy your journey through life. Gratitude helps you feel present in the moment while you build your future with joy and away from negativism.

When you are grateful for what you already have it easy to reflect on all the blessings you enjoy in the present moment and you feel happier and empowered to conquer all your goals. To achieve our goals, we need that inner energy we all have inside, gratitude makes it easier to tap into that energy because you recognize that everything you need to move forward is already inside you. Gratitude brings you strength against any challenges that may lie ahead.

"Wake at dawn with a winged heart and give thanks for another day of loving." — Kahlil Gibran

Gratitude can help you to find happiness

Expressing daily gratitude is a way of living and studies have shown its power to bring happiness to our lives. When we are grateful we feel more satisfied and that feeling of emptiness goes away. We tend to focus on the present when we are grateful instead of focusing on negative thoughts, we feel present, we feel happy to be alive.

Appreciation for what we have right now comes in part from a state of mindfulness that only gratitude can give us. Our brains tend to focus on the bad and negative things and expressing gratitude is a great habit to defeat all those negative feelings and thoughts.

Gratitude creates joy and a lot of positive emotions. Expressing gratitude is good for your mind and great for your soul, you will definitely feel happier once you start practicing gratitude and once you start writing down all your blessings every day.

"The roots of all goodness lie in the soil of appreciation for goodness." — Dalai Lama

Gratitude can improve your health and positivity

The beneficial health effects of writing a gratitude journal have been demonstrated by world leading experts in this subject like Dr. Robert Emmons, a professor of psychology at the University of California. In his studies Dr. Davis and his colleague Michael McCullough from the University of Miami examined the effects of such diaries and journals on almost 200 students.

The students were divided into different groups, one group focused their attention and writings into troubles and annoyances and the other group focused their attention, focus and writing into gratitude.

This experiment showed that the more focused the group was on gratitude the more they started to express feelings of happiness and positivity in contrast with the group that focused on the negative aspects of life.

Why is that? Because what we focus on tends to expand and if we want to expand our health and our positivity we need to start acquiring the habit of writing our blessing daily instead of focusing on the negative aspects of life.

Sounds simple but it doesn't work if we don't practice this habit every day. Don't forget to write down your blessing each day in your gratitude journal and use these beautiful inspiring gratitude quotes included in this book as an inspiration guide.

Gratitude can help you find new relationships

There is definitely a lot of power in our words and saying: "thank you" can open the door to a world of opportunities and new connections. Showing appreciation can help you find new relationships and friends because you will be regarded as a friendly person with a great positive energy. We transmit our energy with our words and with our feelings and the others around us can sense that energy.

The feeling of gratitude simply enhances your empathy with others and it reduces the negative thoughts. Gratitude is an energy connector, an energy enabler that opens more doors and more opportunities to grow and expand your social connections. Gratitude makes you a more sensible person and a more desirable friend.

"Turn your wounds into wisdom." – Oprah Winfrey

Day:_____ Date:__ /__ /__

Today I am Grateful For:

_____

_____

_____

_____

_____

_____

"Dream big and dare to fail." – Norman Vaughan

Day:_____ Date:__ /__ /__

Today I am Grateful For:

_____

_____

_____

_____

_____

Day:_____ Date:__ /__ /__

Today I am Grateful For:

_____

_____

_____

_____

_____

"If there is no struggle, there is no progress." – Frederick Douglass

Day:_____ Date:__ /__ /__

Today I am Grateful For:

_____

_____

_____

_____

Day:_____ Date:__ / __ / __

Today I am Grateful For:

_____
_____
_____
_____
_____
_____

"The purpose of our lives is to be happy." – Dalai Lama

Day:_____ Date:__ / __ / __

Today I am Grateful For:

_____
_____
_____
_____
_____

Day:_____ Date:__ /__ /__

Today I am Grateful For:

_____
_____
_____
_____
_____
_____

"Out of difficulties grow miracles." – Jean de la Bruyere

Day:_____ Date:__ /__ /__

Today I am Grateful For:

_____
_____
_____
_____
_____

Day:_____ Date:__ /__ /__

Today I am Grateful For:

_____
_____
_____
_____
_____
_____

"May the gratitude in my heart kiss all the universe." — Hafiz

Day:_____ Date:__ /__ /__

Today I am Grateful For:

_____
_____
_____
_____
_____

Day:_____ Date:__ /__ /__

Today I am Grateful For:

_____

_____

_____

_____

_____

_____

"The best way to show my gratitude to God is to accept everything, even my problems, with joy." — Mother Teresa

Day:_____ Date:__ /__ /__

Today I am Grateful For:

_____

_____

_____

_____

Day:_____ Date:___ /___ /___

Today I am Grateful For:

_____

_____

_____

_____

_____

_____

"Motivation will almost always beat mere talent." – Norman Ralph
Augustine

Day:_____ Date:___ /___ /___

Today I am Grateful For:

_____

_____

_____

_____

_____

Day: _____ **Date:** __ / __ / __

Today I am Grateful For:

_____

_____

_____

_____

_____

"Learn to be thankful for what you already have, while you pursue all that you want." —Jim Rohn

Day: _____ **Date:** __ / __ / __

Today I am Grateful For:

_____

_____

_____

_____

Day:_____ Date:__ /__ /__

Today I am Grateful For:

_____
_____
_____
_____
_____

"Enjoy the little things, for one day you may look back and realize they were the big things." —Robert Brault

Day:_____ Date:__ /__ /__

Today I am Grateful For:

_____
_____
_____
_____
_____

Day: _____ Date: __ / __ / __

Today I am Grateful For:

_____

_____

_____

_____

_____

"Feeling gratitude and not expressing it is like wrapping a present and not giving it." —William Arthur Ward

Day: _____ Date: __ / __ / __

Today I am Grateful For:

_____

_____

_____

_____

Day:_____ Date:__ /__ /__

Today I am Grateful For:

_____

_____

_____

_____

_____

"The way to develop the best that is in a person is by appreciation and encouragement." —Charles Schwab

Day:_____ Date:__ /__ /__

Today I am Grateful For:

_____

_____

_____

_____

_____

Day:_____ Date:__ /__ /__

Today I am Grateful For:

_____
_____
_____
_____
_____

"When I started counting my blessings, my whole life turned around." —
Willie Nelson

Day:_____ Date:__ /__ /__

Today I am Grateful For:

_____
_____
_____
_____

Day:_____ Date:__ /__ /__

Today I am Grateful For:

_____

_____

_____

_____

_____

"The roots of all goodness lie in the soil of appreciation for goodness." —
Dalai Lama

Day:_____ Date:__ /__ /__

Today I am Grateful For:

_____

_____

_____

_____

Day: _____ **Date:** __ / __ / __

Today I am Grateful For:

_____

_____

_____

_____

_____

"Reflect upon your present blessings, of which every man has plenty; not on your past misfortunes, of which all men have some." —Charles Dickens

Day: _____ **Date:** __ / __ / __

Today I am Grateful For:

_____

_____

_____

_____

_____

Day:_____ Date:__ /__ /__

Today I am Grateful For:

_____

_____

_____

_____

_____

"Some people grumble that roses have thorns; I am grateful that thorns have roses." —Alphonse Karr

Day:_____ Date:__ /__ /__

Today I am Grateful For:

_____

_____

_____

_____

Day:_____ **Date:**__ /__ /__

Today I am Grateful For:

_____

_____

_____

_____

_____

"Gratitude can transform common days into thanksgivings, turn routine jobs into joy and change ordinary opportunities into blessings." – W. A.

Day:_____ **Date:**__ /__ /__

Today I am Grateful For:

_____

_____

_____

_____

_____

*Day:*_____ *Date:*___ /___ /___

Today I am Grateful For:

_____

_____

_____

_____

_____

"Be thankful for what you have; you'll end up having more. If you concentrate on what you don't have, you will never, ever have enough." -- Oprah W.

*Day:*_____ *Date:*___ /___ /___

Today I am Grateful For:

_____

_____

_____

_____

Day:_____ Date:__ /__ /__

Today I am Grateful For:

_____

_____

_____

_____

_____

_____

"Gratitude is not only the greatest of virtues, but the parent of all others." - Marcus Tullius Cicero

Day:_____ Date:__ /__ /__

Today I am Grateful For:

_____

_____

_____

_____

_____

Day:_____ Date:___ /___ /___

Today I am Grateful For:

_____

_____

_____

_____

_____

"The secret to having it all is knowing you already do." - Unknown

Day:_____ Date:___ /___ /___

Today I am Grateful For:

_____

_____

_____

_____

_____

"A grateful heart is a magnet for miracles"

Day:_____ Date:__ /__ /__

Today I am Grateful For:

_____
_____
_____
_____
_____

"The struggle ends when gratitude begins" – Neale Donald Walsh

Day:_____ Date:__ /__ /__

Today I am Grateful For:

_____
_____
_____
_____
_____

Day: _____ Date: __ / __ / __

Today I am Grateful For:

_____

_____

_____

_____

_____

"It is not joy that makes us grateful, it is gratitude that makes us joyful"

Day: _____ Date: __ / __ / __

Today I am Grateful For:

_____

_____

_____

_____

Day:_____ Date:__ /__ /__

Today I am Grateful For:

_____

_____

_____

_____

_____

"Trade your expectations for appreciation and the world changes instantly"
– Tony Robbins

Day:_____ Date:__ /__ /__

Today I am Grateful For:

_____

_____

_____

_____

_____

Day:_____ Date:__ /__ /__

Today I am Grateful For:

_____

_____

_____

_____

_____

"Small seeds of gratitude will produce a harvest of hope"

Day:_____ Date:__ /__ /__

Today I am Grateful For:

_____

_____

_____

_____

Day:_____ Date:__ /__ /__

Today I am Grateful For:

_____

_____

_____

_____

_____

"Start everyday with a grateful heart"

Day:_____ Date:__ /__ /__

Today I am Grateful For:

_____

_____

_____

_____

_____

Day:_____ Date:__ /__ /__

Today I am Grateful For:

_____

_____

_____

_____

_____

"There is always something to be grateful for"

Day:_____ Date:__ /__ /__

Today I am Grateful For:

_____

_____

_____

_____

Day:_____ Date:__ /__ /__

Today I am Grateful For:

_____
_____
_____
_____
_____

"Upon walking let your first thought be, thank you" – Abraham Hicks

Day:_____ Date:__ /__ /__

Today I am Grateful For:

_____
_____
_____
_____

Day:_____ Date:__ / __ / __

Today I am Grateful For:

_____

_____

_____

_____

_____

"I am peaceful, I am Joyful, I am Thankful"

Day:_____ Date:__ / __ / __

Today I am Grateful For:

_____

_____

_____

_____

Day:_____ Date:__ /__ /__

Today I am Grateful For:

_____

_____

_____

_____

_____

_____

"Don't worry. Be happy"

Day:_____ Date:__ /__ /__

Today I am Grateful For:

_____

_____

_____

_____

_____

_____

"All I have is all I need" – May Davis

Day:_____ Date:__ /__ /__

Today I am Grateful For:

_____
_____
_____
_____
_____

"Gratitude is peace" – Anne Lamott

Day:_____ Date:__ /__ /__

Today I am Grateful For:

_____
_____
_____
_____

Day: _____ Date: __ / __ / __

Today I am Grateful For:

_____

_____

_____

_____

_____

_____

"This is a wonderful day. I've never seen this one before" – Maya Angelou

Day: _____ Date: __ / __ / __

Today I am Grateful For:

_____

_____

_____

_____

_____

Day:_____ Date:__ /__ /__

Today I am Grateful For:

_____

_____

_____

_____

_____

"Grateful for where I am now, excited about where I am going"

Day:_____ Date:__ /__ /__

Today I am Grateful For:

_____

_____

_____

_____

Day:_____ Date:__ /__ /__

Today I am Grateful For:

_____
_____
_____
_____
_____

"Always believe smoothing wonderful is about to happen"

Day:_____ Date:__ /__ /__

Today I am Grateful For:

_____
_____
_____
_____
_____

Day:_____ Date:__ /__ /__

Today I am Grateful For:

_____
_____
_____
_____
_____

"Abundance grows from the seed of every thank you" – Mary Davis

Day:_____ Date:__ /__ /__

Today I am Grateful For:

_____
_____
_____
_____
_____

Day:_____ Date:__ /__ /__

Today I am Grateful For:

_____

_____

_____

_____

_____

"I do small things with great love" – Mother Theresa

Day:_____ Date:__ /__ /__

Today I am Grateful For:

_____

_____

_____

_____

Day:_____ Date:__ /__ /__

Today I am Grateful For:

_____
_____
_____
_____
_____

"If the only prayer you ever say is "Thank You", that will be enough –Eckhart Tolle

Day:_____ Date:__ /__ /__

Today I am Grateful For:

_____
_____
_____
_____

Day:_____ Date:__ /__ /__

Today I am Grateful For:

_____
_____
_____
_____
_____

"A moment of gratitude makes a difference in your attitude"

Day:_____ Date:__ /__ /__

Today I am Grateful For:

_____
_____
_____
_____

Day:_____ Date:__ /__ /__

Today I am Grateful For:

_____

_____

_____

_____

_____

_____

"Be present in all things and thankful for all things" – Maya Angelou Picasso

Day:_____ Date:__ /__ /__

Today I am Grateful For:

_____

_____

_____

_____

_____

Express yourself with this coloring page

"Be thankful for another day, not everybody made it, so don't take it for granted"

Day:_____ Date:__ /__ /__

Today I am Grateful For:

_____

_____

_____

_____

_____

"Gratitude is when memory is stored in the heart and not in the mind" –
Lionel Hampton

Day:_____ Date:__ /__ /__

Today I am Grateful For:

_____

_____

_____

_____

Day: _____ **Date:** __ / __ / __

Today I am Grateful For:

_____

_____

_____

_____

_____

"Be thankful for all the troubles that you don't have"

Day: _____ **Date:** __ / __ / __

Today I am Grateful For:

_____

_____

_____

_____

Day:_____ Date:__ /__ /__

Today I am Grateful For:

_____

_____

_____

_____

_____

"I am perfect as I am and I am thankful for who I am"

Day:_____ Date:__ /__ /__

Today I am Grateful For:

_____

_____

_____

_____

Day: _____ Date: __ / __ / __

Today I am Grateful For:

_____

_____

_____

_____

_____

"Gratitude is the best medicine, it heals your mind, your body and your spirit and attracts more things to be grateful for"

Day: _____ Date: __ / __ / __

Today I am Grateful For:

_____

_____

_____

_____

_____

Day:_____ Date:__ /__ /__

Today I am Grateful For:

_____

_____

_____

_____

_____

"Have an attitude of gratitude" – Thomas S. Monson

Day:_____ Date:__ /__ /__

Today I am Grateful For:

_____

_____

_____

_____

_____

Day:_____ Date:__ /__ /__

Today I am Grateful For:

_____

_____

_____

_____

_____

"Everything you can imagine is real" – Pablo Picasso

Day:_____ Date:__ /__ /__

Today I am Grateful For:

_____

_____

_____

_____

Day:_____ Date:__ /__ /__

Today I am Grateful For:

_____

_____

_____

_____

_____

"Thankful, grateful, blessed"

Day:_____ Date:__ /__ /__

Today I am Grateful For:

_____

_____

_____

_____

_____

Day:_____ Date:__ /__ /__

Today I am Grateful For:

_____

_____

_____

_____

_____

"Interrupt anxiety with gratitude"

Day:_____ Date:__ /__ /__

Today I am Grateful For:

_____

_____

_____

_____

_____

Day: _____ **Date:** __ / __ / __

Today I am Grateful For:

_____

_____

_____

_____

_____

"When you are grateful fear disappears and abundance appears" – Tony Robbins

Day: _____ **Date:** __ / __ / __

Today I am Grateful For:

_____

_____

_____

_____

_____

"Gratitude paints little smiley faces in everything it touches" –
Richelle Goodrich

Day:_____ Date:__ /__ /__

Today I am Grateful For:

_____

_____

_____

_____

_____

"Gratitude opens your heart to love"

Day:_____ Date:__ /__ /__

Today I am Grateful For:

_____

_____

_____

_____

_____

Day:_____ Date:__ /__ /__

Today I am Grateful For:

_____

_____

_____

_____

_____

"Gratitude is the vitamin of the soul"

Day:_____ Date:__ /__ /__

Today I am Grateful For:

_____

_____

_____

_____

Day:_____ Date:__ /__ /__

Today I am Grateful For:

_____

_____

_____

_____

_____

"Everything you can imagine is real" – Pablo Picasso

Day:_____ Date:__ /__ /__

Today I am Grateful For:

_____

_____

_____

_____

Day: _____ Date: __ / __ / __

Today I am Grateful For:

_____

_____

_____

_____

_____

"Breathe, Relax, Let Go"

Day: _____ Date: __ / __ / __

Today I am Grateful For:

_____

_____

_____

_____

Day:_____ Date:__ /__ /__

Today I am Grateful For:

_____

_____

_____

_____

_____

"I am grateful of the blessings I receive daily"

Day:_____ Date:__ /__ /__

Today I am Grateful For:

_____

_____

_____

_____

Day:_____ Date:__ /__ /__

Today I am Grateful For:

_____

_____

_____

_____

_____

_____

"Gratitude is the sign of noble souls" – Aesop

Day:_____ Date:__ /__ /__

Today I am Grateful For:

_____

_____

_____

_____

Day:_____ Date:___ /___ /___

Today I am Grateful For:

_____

_____

_____

_____

_____

"Begin each day with a grateful heart"

Day:_____ Date:___ /___ /___

Today I am Grateful For:

_____

_____

_____

_____

Day:_____ Date:__ /__ /__

Today I am Grateful For:

_____

_____

_____

_____

_____

"Gratitude and attitude are not challenges; they are choices" – Robert Braathe

Day:_____ Date:__ /__ /__

Today I am Grateful For:

_____

_____

_____

_____

*Day:*_____ *Date:*__ /__ /__

Today I am Grateful For:

_____

_____

_____

_____

_____

"Gratitude is the best attitude"

*Day:*_____ *Date:*__ /__ /__

Today I am Grateful For:

_____

_____

_____

_____

Express yourself with this coloring page

"Gratitude is riches. Complaint is poverty" – Doris Day

Day:_____ Date:___ /___ /___

Today I am Grateful For:

_____

_____

_____

_____

_____

"I am grateful for the waterfall of amazing blessings in my life"

Day:_____ Date:___ /___ /___

Today I am Grateful For:

_____

_____

_____

_____

_____

Day:_____ Date:___ /___ /___

Today I am Grateful For:

_____

_____

_____

_____

_____

"There is no joy without gratitude" – Brene Brown

Day:_____ Date:___ /___ /___

Today I am Grateful For:

_____

_____

_____

_____

Day:_____ Date:__ /__ /__

Today I am Grateful For:

_____
_____
_____
_____
_____

"Gratitude will shift you to a higher frequency, and you will attract much better things

Day:_____ Date:__ /__ /__

Today I am Grateful For:

_____
_____
_____
_____

Day:_____ Date:__ /__ /__

Today I am Grateful For:

_____

_____

_____

_____

_____

"Gratitude opens the heart and creates space for love and joy"

Day:_____ Date:__ /__ /__

Today I am Grateful For:

_____

_____

_____

_____

_____